Who's That on My

by Aviva Williams

I am a fish and I live in the sea,
It's called the Sea of Galilee,
Sometimes it's calm and the waves are smooth,
But then, storms come and the waves are huge.

One night it was stormy and the thunder roared,
A ship was sailing with men on board,
And as they were struggling to sail through the night,
I heard someone yelling in terror and fright.

I swam to the surface and lifted my head,
To see what was causing the men to dread,
The men were standing, looking over the sea,
And pointing at something fearfully.

Coming towards them I clearly saw,
A man on the water - I opened my jaw!
Was it really a man walking over the sea?
Not sinking, not drowning, how could this be?

Was it a trick? A man can't float,
Was I mistaken and had He a boat?
But no, I saw Him walk by me,
His feet on the surface of the stormy sea.

The seas were rough, the waves were high,
Yet as He walked His feet were dry,
And from the ship the men cried out,
"It is a ghost without a doubt!"

Then piercing through the wind and noise,
Came the most majestic voice,
"Be not afraid. Be of good cheer.
It's Me - Jesus - have no fear."

One man, Peter, called out madly,
"Jesus if that's You, I'll gladly,
Climb overboard and come to You,
And walk on water with You too."

Jesus said, "Come on the water,"
And he stepped out without a falter,
And everyone gasped for miraculously,
Peter stood up on top of the sea!

Looking at Jesus, he boldly stepped,
And all the while afloat he kept,
Then the waves began to rise,
And Peter stopped and moved his eyes.

No longer looking at Jesus' face,
Peter looked at the crashing waves,
He panicked with fear and looked around,
Then felt his feet sinking down.

"Help me!" he cried, "I'm drowning fast,
My walk on the water didn't last!"
As quick as a flash, Jesus came,
And lifted him up and called his name.

"Peter! Peter! Why did you doubt?
I'm right here to pull you out.
You should have kept your eyes on Me,
Not on the storm or on the sea."

And together they walked back to the ship,
Jesus holding Peter so he did not slip,
And then when they were back on board,
The storm just stopped and was no more.

The men worshiped Jesus and fell to the floor,
"You are the Son of God for sure,
The Miracle-worker, the Great I Am,
Our Messiah, Deliverer, the Precious Lamb."

And Jesus replied with such love and grace,
"Peter you needed to gaze on My face,
For if you'd kept your eyes on Me,
You would have walked across this sea."

I stayed and watched as the ship sailed away,
What a miracle I had seen that day,
But more than that, I had seen,
Jesus, my Creator, walk by me!

And still today, Jesus says the same,
To all His children who love His Name,
"No matter what you see or hear,
Just trust in Me and do not fear.

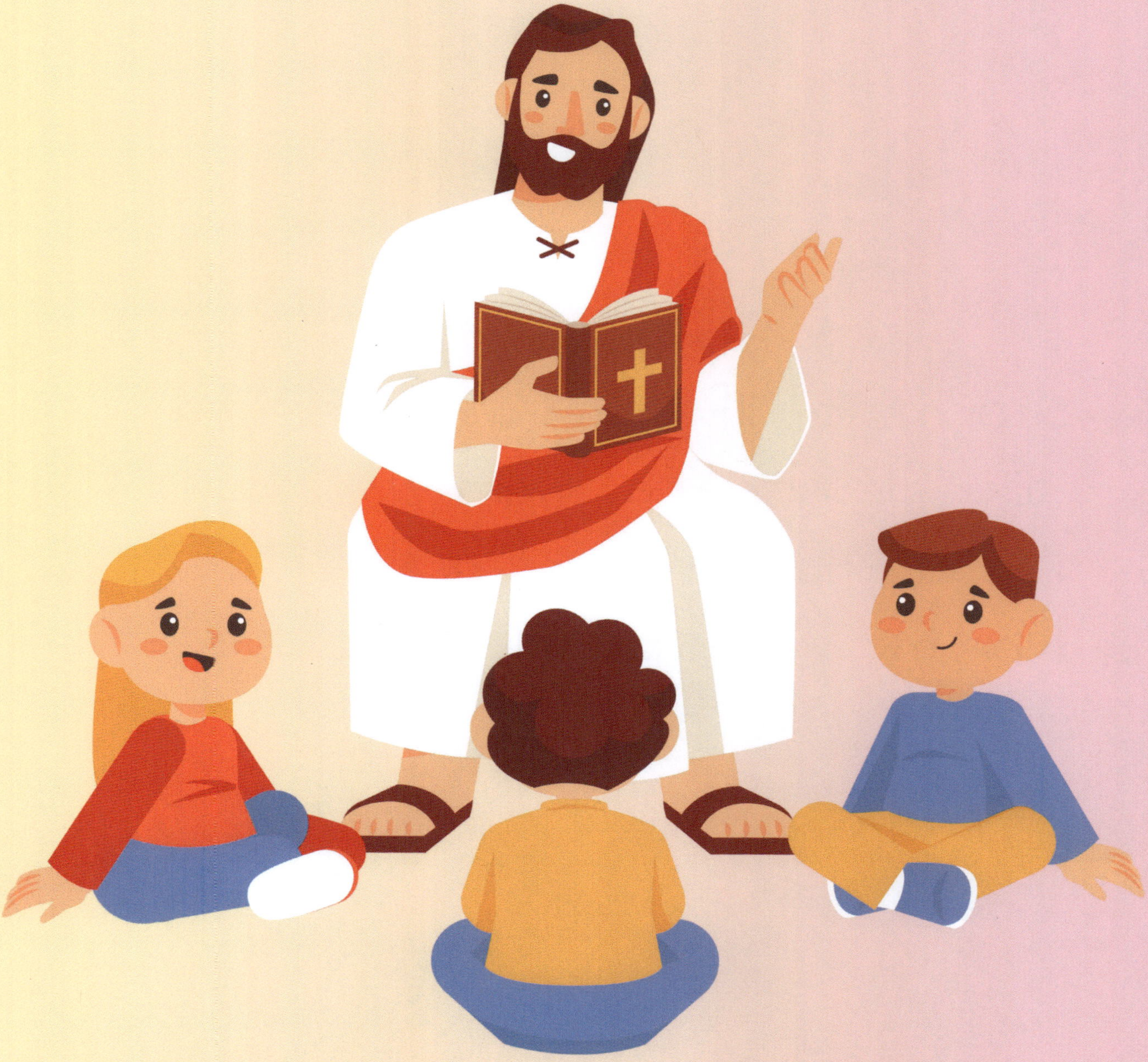

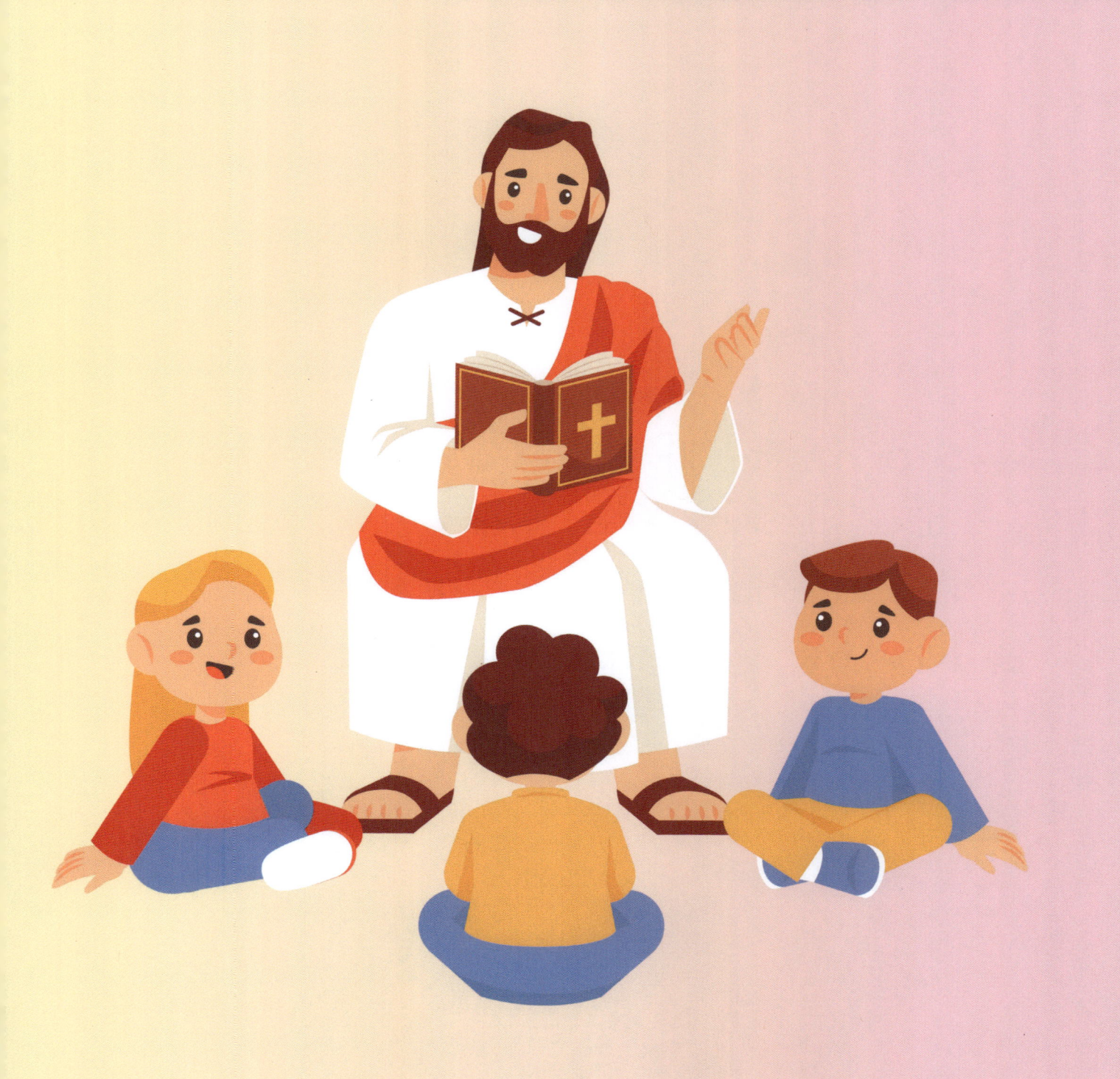

Storms of life may come to you,
But do not fret, I am with you,
Situations may arise,
But on my Word just keep your eyes.

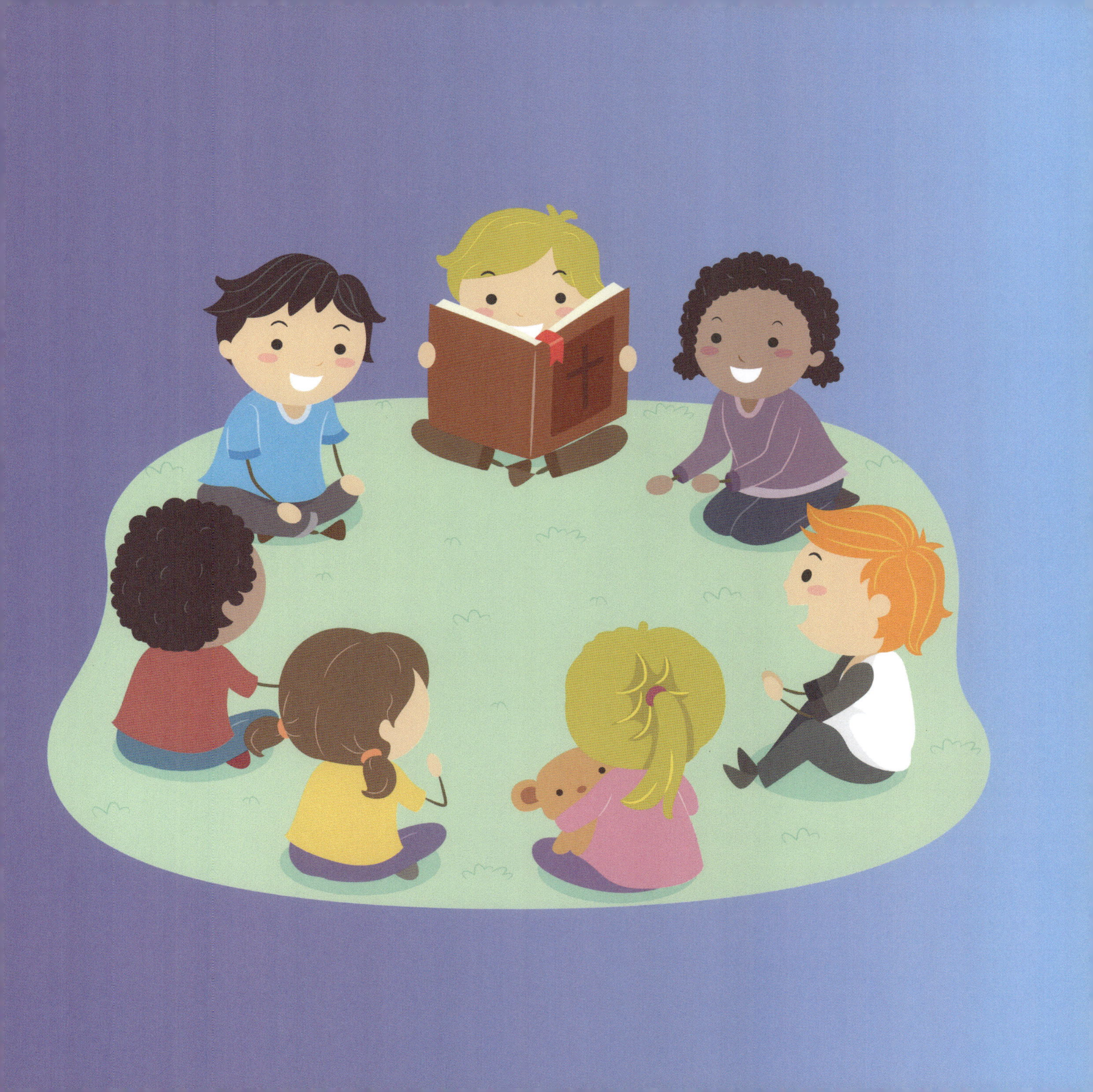

Hear My voice and learn to obey,
Trust My Word and don't turn away,
Each day be faithful and listen to Me,
And don't be distracted by what you see.

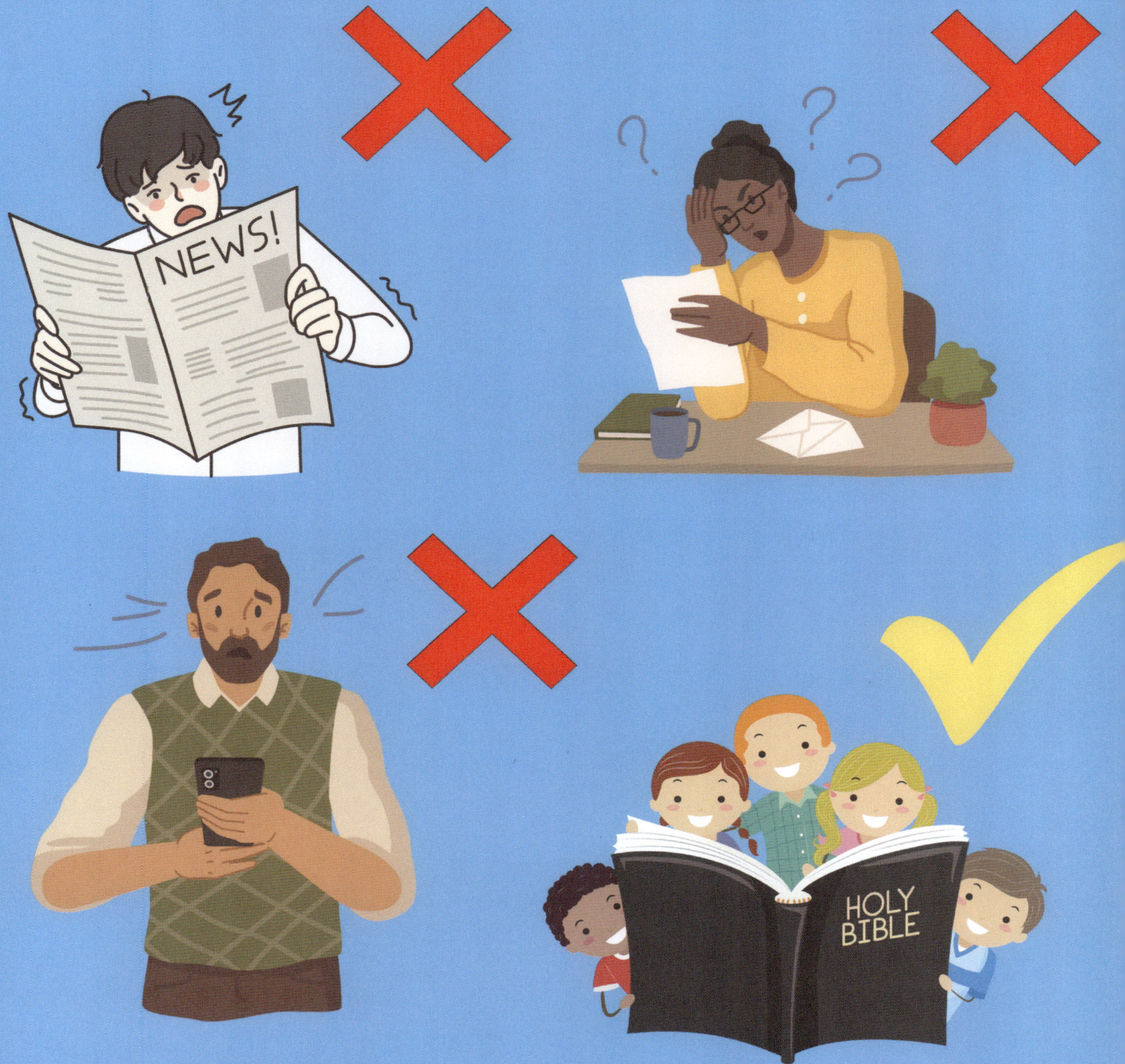
NEWS!
HOLY BIBLE

Together we will walk on through,
Every problem that comes to you,
And you will walk in victory,
As long as you keep your eyes on Me."

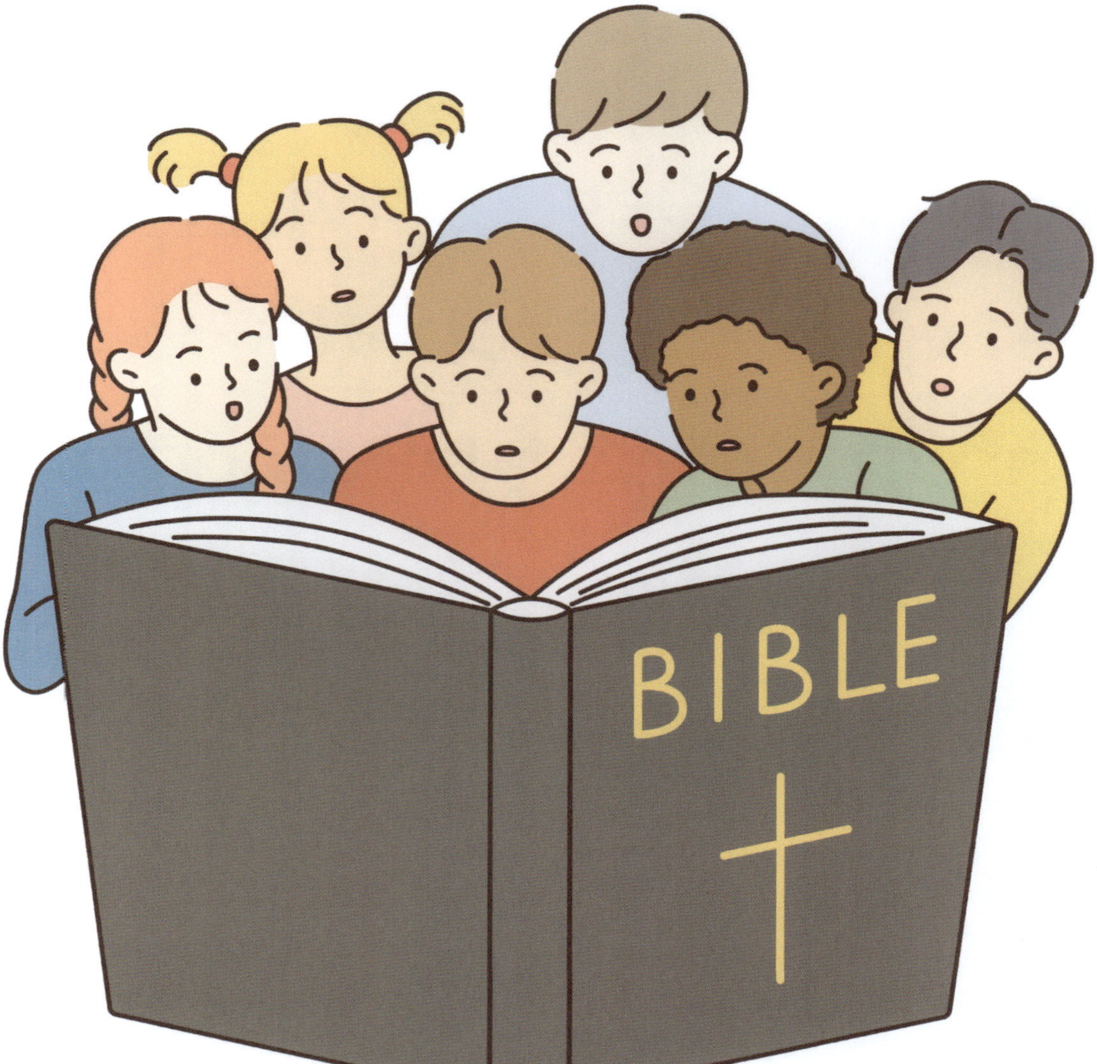
BIBLE

Prayer

Thank You Jesus that You are always with me. You take care of me and protect me. Thank you that as I obey You and Your Word, I will not fear, I will not lack and I will have joy and peace.

Prayer of Salvation

Do you know that God loves you and He has a special plan for your life?

God sent His Son, Jesus, to come to live on the earth, and then die on the Cross, shedding His Blood to pay the price for our sin. Jesus then rose from the dead and He lives forevermore. The Bible tells us that if we ask Him into our hearts to be our Lord and Savior, and we believe that He rose from the dead, we will be forgiven, and be filled with His Holy Spirit - the Bible calls this being "born-again". Our lives can be blessed and have His joy, peace, health, prosperity and protection every day. We can follow the plan He has for our lives and then, one day, we will also go and live with Him in Heaven forever. It's His gift to us.

The Bible tells us that this gift is for anyone who calls on the Name of Jesus - and this includes YOU! I pray that the Lord will bless you and your family, with long and healthy lives. I ask that Jesus, makes Himself real to you and does a quick work in your heart, that if you have not received Jesus as your Lord and Savior, I pray that you will do so right now.

If you would like to receive the gift that God has for you today, say this prayer out loud, and mean it from your heart:

"Dear Lord Jesus, come into my heart. Forgive me of my sin. Set me free. Change me. Jesus, I thank You that You died for me. I believe that You are risen from the dead and that You're coming back again for me. Fill me with the Holy Spirit. Give me boldness to tell others about You. I'm saved. I'm born-again. I'm forgiven. I'm on my way to Heaven because I have Jesus in my heart forever. Amen."

Printed in Great Britain
by Amazon